THIS JOURNAL BELONGS TO

_____

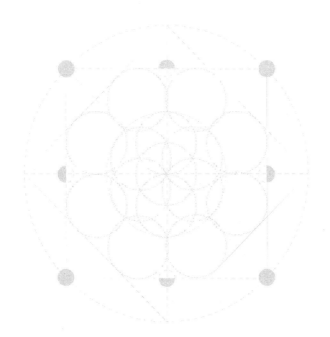

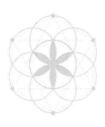

INTRODUCTION

In the beginning, was the word. This truth, recognised in traditions from East to West, acknowledges sound as a primary creative force, second only to the vast spaciousness from which it arises.

Through my work as a healer, I began to realise the implications of working with sound, particularly the medicinal vibrations of mantra. The beauty and effectiveness of working with light cannot be denied, but when sound is also integrated into a practice, the amplification of healing is remarkable.

Our capacity to heal ourselves and our planet increases radically—some may say miraculously—when we engage the three parts of our being the Tibetan Buddhists recognise and articulate as body, mind and speech.

From prayer to prophesy and blessing to clearing, your voice is a powerful gift. In Eastern esotericism, it is considered an authentic manifestation of your unique energy signature. There are tones and nuances in vocal expression beyond that of having a pleasant speaking or singing voice. Your voice's spiritual power is less about exoteric sound and more about its esoteric effect on yourself and others. The voice is a powerful means of soul-to-soul communication. It is capable of healing, soothing, strengthening and awakening. You can express yourself through words and sound, but the intention and quality of energy within your voice—the quality of your spiritual integration—can heal. Beautiful words with no heart behind them hold little power, yet simple words imbued with intention and energy from the heart can profoundly alleviate suffering.

White light is polychromatic, meaning it holds all the colours we need for healing ourselves, each other and our planet and her many precious creatures. Frequencies within each colour can be metabolised for functions, such as purification, strengthening and awakening — rather like multivitamins for the soul. Those frequencies can be recognised and received by the soul and heard by the soul's inner ear.

When we add sound to our practices, through voice or mantra, a powerful integration occurs between body, speech and mind—i.e. across all facets and dimensions of our multidimensional being. The result of this is healing, transformation and rapid progress toward spiritual bliss and freedom. White light frequencies are powerful as they integrate light and its sound frequencies for awakening.

The loving and divine intelligence of white light frequencies equips the soul to end negative thought and behaviour. It transforms the soul, so we become stronger and wiser, capable of rapturous delight and connected to our true life path. As the sound-infused light fills and heals us, we are being prepared as spiritual channels. The light can then flow through us into all dimensions for the spiritual benefit of all beings.

As we make an emotional heart connection with the realms of light, we internalise and integrate the divine beauty they emanate. Eventually, we radiate this beauty for the benefit of all beings, and our mind becomes more luminous and increasingly enlightened.

As the mind engages with light, it becomes capable of recognising it beyond appearance. No longer does it believe in the illusion of matter as devoid of light. The mind begins to realise, respect and journey with light within the body. In time, if absorption is deep enough, you will start to experience the vast space—and light and sound that spontaneously arise from that—within the body. You will come to see your body for its beautiful potential as a divine instrument.

In Tibetan tradition, there are stories of spiritual masters who became so infused with light through their spiritual practices that their bodies took on a translucent quality and ceased to cast a shadow. I had a powerful experience in a deep meditation, where I realised my bones were comprised entirely of light and floating in space inside my body. "We are truly more light than matter," floated through my mind. It was a gentle yet ecstatic experience, one of many, where I have realised the inner depths of being and how truly divine and miraculous our bodies are—not only for their physical genius but for their spiritual radiance.

That brief experience in meditation was so unexpectedly and radically purifying that it unleashed an intense, life-changing healing process which took over two years to work through. A mere glimpse of the inner truth of light within, for a matter of seconds, was enough to uproot something that had withstood decades of inner work. The realisation of light within is one facet of self-realisation. It is profoundly purifying, protective, empowering and healing.

The body's genius knows how and when to reveal its true nature. Your soul naturally integrates and refines itself as a divine instrument as you journey along your spiritual path, realising the qualities of body, speech and mind. The quality of your voice evolves in that process.

Regardless of whether you will ever hit diva heights in a recording studio, or discover a career as a voice-over artist, as you evolve spiritually, the subtle power of your voice becomes increasingly infused with light and many beautiful things happen as a result. The spontaneous effects can include creating healing for others and more effortlessly attracting and magnifying beautiful realisations within yourself and your life. That which cannot sustain the higher vibration of being that you are now beginning to manifest will also be healed. As you work with white light frequencies, the quality of your instrument changes. So too does the spiritual purity of sound that emerges with increasing potential to benefit all beings.

As you awaken, your voice can become a means by which you energetically contribute to the co-creation of a new system. You may be a birth mother or founding father of a more consciously integrated human culture. In Tibetan understanding, speech is not limited to what we say but includes an esoteric vibration. What we think, how we work with our energies, what we do and what we say are all communicated. Speech is our entire being in expression, in manifestation.

To find your voice in this profound way, you need to find yourself—not the ideas of yourself that you likely grew up believing, nor the projections others attribute to you (Although, that recognition can be enormously liberating!). Realising our true innate self is a process. Some practices support that process, and others inhibit it. To access sacred and authentic voice, we need to take the short yet astonishingly in-depth journey of dropping from head to heart and heart to belly, to connect all three.

Voice is intimately connected to the body, the instrument through which it manifests. So this journey entails learning to love, trust and discover the inner spiritual reality of your body. There is an extraordinary universe of fathomless divinity within. The body is the temple through which we can recognise, receive and honour the sacred radiance that pervades all creation.

This journal was crafted to help you connect with and integrate the three key aspects of your being:

— the vast creativity and resourcefulness of limitless mind,

— the spacious interiority of genius that is your body,

— and the liberating energetic potency of your healing voice.

You can further explore these facets in the companion creations, *White Light Oracle*, *White Light Frequencies*, and *White Light Frequencies Healing*™. Remember, no matter what tools support your journey, it is your own inner spiritual beauty that you are discovering.

As each one of us connects with these divinely gifted dimensions of being, may our awakening generate spiritual benefit for all beings. May we heal, awaken, play, sing, speak and discover, together.

Namaste,

Alana x

*Through unconditional love, wisdom, peace and compassion, I ask for
healing for myself and all beings so that the divine truth of grace may
manifest for the greatest good.*

Trust in what your heart yearns for without concern about how it will manifest. That which may appear to be out of reach or unavailable to you is closer than you realise.

Soul-deep attraction inspires us to be open, passionate and willing to engage with life, other people and new, vitalising pathways and practices that inspire us. Allow your heart to be enchanted as you embrace your unique journey.

I open my heart to divine wisdom. I ask for unconditional love and the highest levels of white light available to me to enter my heart. In this sacred space, I discover and express my unique voice.

I open to grace, healing, protection and blessing.

As you let go of known worlds and reach for the unfamiliar, the call of the heart can feel liberating but unsettling. Following such a path will bring a fresh influx of energy and expand your understanding of yourself, your life path and your higher purpose. It is meant to be.

A path is opening up for you. When your heart leaps at the prospect of it, know something extraordinary is unfolding. Trust where your heart is leading you.

Things are working out in their own way. Spirit wants to bring you a blessing and a resolution, but you must let go and allow it to happen.

Events are unfolding according to a higher plan. Even when your plans go awry,
know that all will come together at the right time and in the best way possible.
Surrender your struggle and hold on to your faith.

You do not need to be in control to be safe and have things work out
in the best possible way.

What message does your authentic soul voice wish to share with you now?

The authentic mystical experience of divine love is not just emotional —
it is transfiguring. It awakens us to the beauty of divine light within.

A beautiful and uplifting outcome is being offered to you.
Trust in Spirit, let go and receive.

Bhavana is a Sanskrit word that means infusion. Allow white light to gently infuse into your being like a sacred tea, subtly perfuming and enriching your soul. Intend to release any concerns into the light, now. Let go from your heart. In the light, your worries can dissolve and transform.

I embrace my voice as an authentic expression of my unique energetic signature.

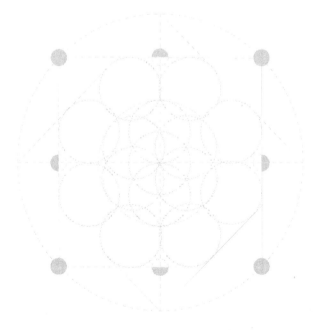

You can give up your faith in the ways of the world, and instead, trust in the ways of Spirit, unconditionally. Believe in the power of Spirit to show you the way through all troubles with tenderness and mercy.

When you trust your courage more than your doubt, you will be ready to listen to Spirit and act on what you perceive. You will be capable, willing and ready to live as a light on this Earth.

_I choose to trust in the unfolding of a higher loving plan in my life,
the divine timing of that plan and my capacity to respond and act
with wisdom. I have the courage to continue. I have every right to be
confident in myself and trusting of Spirit._

Do not give up, but allow your heart to disengage from your struggles.
Give yourself much-needed rest. Commit yourself to your sacred
journey and relax, trusting that the right thing
will happen at the right time.

Restore yourself through the recognition of your spiritual beauty,
value and presence. In the space of restful immersion,
you realise you are enough and discover peace.

Rest for as long as you need.

Powerful, subtle energies are helping ensure your success. Believe that many positive synchronicities and unexpected allies will rally to support you.

*Spirit works with tremendous subtlety, even when accomplishing a
masterful stroke of luminous inspiration and powerful grace. You may not
be fully aware of the divine protection being granted or of negativity that
was averted, yet you are being held in grace.*

SOUND CLEARING TECHNIQUE

Sound is steeped in healing potential. When we utilise not only sound, but sacred sound known as mantra, we access a powerful, intentional acoustic medicine for awakening, healing and liberation. Our sound clearing techniques can then become acts of compassionate wisdom that create benefit for many beings in many dimensions.

The desire to offer to heal and activate energy flow can be noble, particularly when applied to our self-healing. We can sometimes project our frustration at the seeming lack of results in our lives onto the world or another person. We may want to activate or heal them (or places on the earth) when what we need to do is accept our feelings of helplessness and go through the growth required to cultivate patience, wisdom, compassion and courage in greater measure.

When we see a problem, we typically want to fix it. That is sensible unless we fall into the trap of believing we have the right, or even the duty, to change others to facilitate the solution we think is best. That belief can lead us into a game of blame, manipulation and underestimation of the creative and spiritual potential within all beings. Good intentions can all too easily deliver less than desirable outcomes.

We cannot always know how or why someone's suffering is unfolding as it is. Perhaps they are reaching the low-point necessary for them to let go of a very stubborn ego-pattern. In that breakdown, there could be a gloriously freeing breakthrough that is imminent. Our compassionate hearts would not wish suffering on any being, yet our wisdom mind understands there is a higher loving purpose behind all things.

Whilst we can work toward awakening compassion within, we need wisdom too. One of the best ways to align with wisdom is to work with a mantra that holds divine knowledge and can operate most effectively. Compassion compels us to create positive, liberating energies for all beings, and mantra allows us to do so with wisdom. We can work with mantra as medicine and allow its innate wisdom to provide what is needed.

Although there are different mantras for different purposes, at a very high level of understanding, all mantras are one. Any mantra delivered with complete awareness is a whole universe of healing and liberation. So we can focus on the simple mantras below and work with them with an open and trusting heart, knowing that the mantra will unveil its wisdom to us.

When we work with sacred sound such as mantra, we want to recognise that it is a powerful divine tool and needs to be expressed with care. You might feel disrupted by a noisy (even if well-meaning) intrusion into your life, so too, our well-intentioned actions may cause unnecessary disturbance to many beings including other humans or nature spirits, for example. Given humanity's population, this is part of life, and developing tolerance and compassion is essential. However, if we want to work with mantras and intentional sound clearing, we also need to develop sensitivity and skilfulness. Otherwise, our attempts to create peace may agitate already overstimulated beings, increasing rather than alleviating disturbances.

I have heard stories of attempted spirit clearings that resulted in more problems for all concerned. The spirit beings causing the issues were disturbed, rather than healed, by the process. The intentions of the healer were undoubtedly to be of assistance. However, they approached the task intending to mould the environment to how they thought it should be. Through that covert aggression, the outcome was not so good for anyone.

It is not our job to control the energies around us. Our spiritual task is to learn to accept what is and grow our capacity to respond to life with skill through self-healing and spiritual awakening. As we grow, our natural influence can expand organically. We can offer and share our awareness, rather than attempt to control others. To dispense with attempts at control is to give another permission to take responsibility for their life, and free ourselves from the burden of judgement. Spontaneously arising from this is increased freedom for all involved.

This practice focuses on clearing your field and your immediate environment into which your energy will naturally expand. You can use this to clear spaces when you travel but remember to practise with gentleness and grace, never force. You have the will, and the permission, to secure your energy field. You do not need any kind of violence to enact that right when you realise your innate permission to recalibrate your energy field. That there is a natural and spontaneous positive effect for the energies around you is a bonus!

THE TECHNIQUE

You may like to work with silence or to play a piece of music that resonates for your particular state of being at this time. That may especially be the case if there is a lot of distraction or noise around you, and you are finding it difficult to drop into the spaciousness beneath the noise. A piece of music may give you something else to focus upon, and if that music feels sacred to you, it can create space rather than add more noise.

Stand or sit comfortably. Connect with your heart. To do this, you may like to place a hand on your heart and take several moments to become very present.

Sense your energy field. You may be aware of it already, or it may be new for you. A generalised sense of your energy field as existing beyond your physical body to some degree is enough. You can play with expanding your energy field on an exhalation and retracting it somewhat on an inhalation if you wish. Then let your energy field, and your sense of it, settle.

Drop your shoulders and feel your connection to the earth through your feet. Sense your energetic connection to yourself growing stronger from within as if the central channel of your spine is awakening and shining radiant energy out in all directions to strengthen you on every level. Feel, sense or intend that you are becoming stronger and more stable from within. You may wish to close your eyes to allow this process for as long as necessary.

Sense your energy radiating from your heart and dispersing freely through your being, shining in all directions like an inner spiritual sun. Let it be gentle yet powerful.

If you can, focus on the spaciousness within the sound of the music you are playing or the spaciousness within the silence if you are fortunate enough to practice in relative quiet.

Become aware of the spaciousness within your energy field. Matter contains space. The spaciousness is there; we just need to learn to drop into it. Relax, and allow your heart to open softly and gently into vast, restful spaciousness.

Much of what requires clearing will dissolve or self-liberate into that spaciousness. You do not need to focus on or hold on to anything. Continue to drop into the spaciousness as you allow your awareness to open and expand into it.

When you are ready, you can hold an intention to send a blessing of clearing and protection, which will also infuse and seal your energy field with high-level frequencies. The greater your sense of spaciousness, the greater your receptivity to the sound and effect of this mantra. Simply allow your energy field to receive and vibrate with it.

Gently, from the heart, utter the cleansing, blessing and protective three-syllable mantra below. You can say it in Sanskrit or Tibetan, or both—the alternate spellings are below. You can repeat the mantra three, seven, nine, eighteen, twenty-one, or more times as you wish. Count the repetitions with your heart, rather than your head, so you remain relaxed and surrendered to the sound.

OM AH HUM

OM AH HUNG

You can visualise, imagine or intend that the mantra's sounds are swirling in a beautiful spiral within and around you, gracefully and gently moving through your energy field, awakening spiritual benefit of all beings.

When you are ready, you can complete the process with this prayer:

May all beings be blessed with divine grace, freed from suffering and awakened into divine compassion. So be it.

Finish with your hands in prayer at your heart.

Take a few moments to ground yourself. Sense the boundaries of your physical self, your skin, and the connection of your body to a physical object (such as the floor or chair) to anchor yourself back in the here and now.

You have completed your process.

*Divine grace assumes whatever form will benefit the spiritual seeker
to ensure their continued progress and facilitate the right things at the
right time. All you need do is invite it into your heart and trust.*

Our spiritual practices are our life raft when the oceans of life become wild and our magic carpet when we feel stuck and need inspiration and freedom. Our practices increase our compassion for ourselves and others.

The ideas that nurture and inspire your heart are important, and the actions that transform hesitation, fear and doubt into boldness, trust and confidence are essential to bringing those ideas to life.

You can express your truth with kindness and mercy, as an act of gentle freedom,
without needing to impose it upon another.

You can now feel sweet relief through the knowledge that Spirit is with you
and wants you to heal any matter that concerns you.

Choose your thoughts and words, so they reflect what you truly wish to put out into the world because your influence is stronger and further reaching than you realise.

You shall know what you need to know when you need to know it and find your way in truth.

You are blessed. You are granted a unique, unrepeatable human life.
Even if you believe in reincarnation, acknowledging the soul continues to
grow over many lifetimes, there will only be one life when you are this you.

*When you treasure this life, you will become bolder, more fearless,
more willing to step up as your real self, more prepared to engage in
healing and more ready to say yes to what makes your heart sing.*

Entrust the spiritual progress and protection of all beings to the capable heart of
the divine feminine, as you care for yourself and others as consciously as you can.

Recognise that the light is intelligent and knows what you need and when.
It is bringing an abundance of offerings to you, in the perfect way and at
the perfect time. This will help you relax further and let go.

Gently but firmly cast aside that which does not resonate as being true for your heart.

All prayers are answered at the perfect time and in the perfect way.

You have a powerful voice, which can foster healing and wisdom on our planet.

Holy ones, great ones, beings of divine light and healing,
I call upon your enlightened wisdom and compassion to
support my soul in releasing the constraints that have
distorted and silenced my authentic voice. I accept my
voice entirely—from the way it sounds to how I speak and
the truths I have stood for in this and other lifetimes. I
release all vows, impediments and conditions that hinder
the awakening of my authentic voice as I align with the
great compassion that holds space and wisdom for healing.
Beloved ones, please bless my voice with your divine
protection as I embrace the uniqueness of my energy and in
doing so, facilitate my spiritual awakening for the spiritual
benefit of all beings.

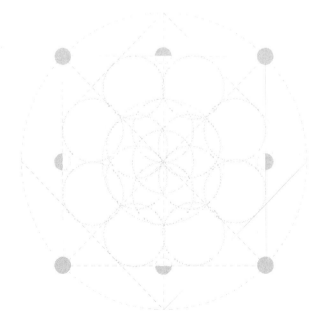

A more authentic, awakened you is coming to life.

Do not give your power away, but do trust in the greater guiding wisdom
at work in all aspects of your life.

Ask for help from enlightened spiritual beings for any matter of concern and help shall be granted.

Believe all problems can be resolved, and a more graceful life
experience is opening up for you, now.

Sometimes, you may feel limited by stereotypes, but your true nature can never be restricted or controlled. Embrace the journey of what it feels like to be you, in your own body and the deeper experience of the absolute freedom of your spirit.

Every soul has a unique path and the spiritual blessing of freedom to pursue it.

The feminine energies in every soul empower our ability to embrace what is and find compassion, which generates mercy, forgiveness, wisdom, and evolution.

The masculine energies in every soul encourage exploration, development and enquiry, leading to discernment and higher understanding so that negativities are banished from our personal space before they can undermine our healing and spiritual progress.

Your inner and outer scars are marks of your soul's courage.
They are signs of strength, survival and your willingness to be alive.

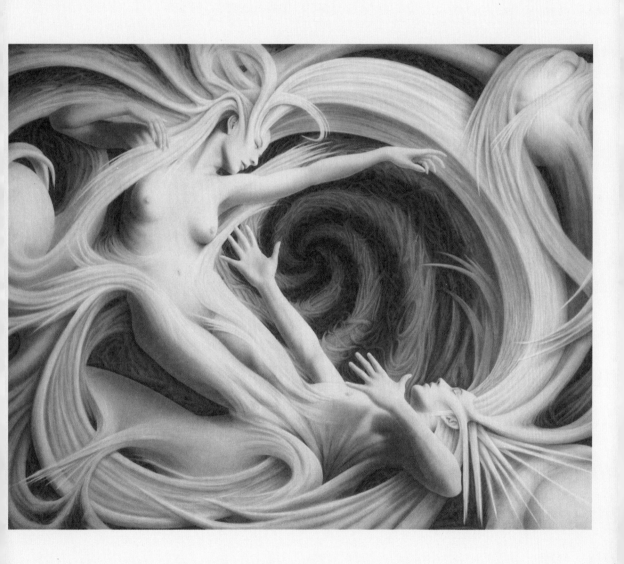

SOUL BLUEPRINT ACTIVATION

Many people believe their life purpose can be reduced to a job. Although meaningful work can be an important part of our life journey, a job is not our purpose. Our purpose is to self-realise, and our soul blueprint knows how to accomplish this. Our soul blueprint is the original spiritual plan for our development. It is the innate guiding wisdom within each being that knows what it is meant to be, and the superior pathway for awakening that potential for the maximum spiritual benefit of all.

When we are in touch with our deep inner truth, we live by that blueprint. It holds a feeling of resonance, validity and authenticity for us. Through its blessings, and preordained challenges that help us grow, living by this inner spiritual directive strengthens, inspires and ultimately creates joyful self-actualisation.

An example of the soul blueprint in action is the intelligence within a caterpillar that knows how to move with patience and engage in an astonishingly dramatic transformation process, to emerge as a butterfly.

The original and purposeful wisdom of our true spiritual nature is life-changing. It can dissolve inherited pains and psychological struggles and allow projections from others (which may influence us, yet are about their desires, not our true nature) to cease to affect us. Under the soul blueprint's influence, we embrace our unique life path and discover who we are according to our unique path and divine timing.

Rather like the radical and courageous alchemy of the caterpillar, there will be moments on your authentic life path, in absolute harmony with your divine destiny as prescribed in your soul blueprint, when you will feel disoriented or conflicted or confused. It may be that a difficult choice is before you, or that your life feels as though it is spinning into chaos.

During such moments, remember the innate genius of that soul totem, the tiny caterpillar. The same spiritual intelligence that will guide its evolution, guides all beings, including you. In that sense, we are never alone.

Every sentient being is on an evolutionary journey that unfolds according to guiding wisdom with love as its essence. This process can sometimes be intimidating, but it is trustworthy. In the fulfilment of that process, which is complete self-actualisation and radiant self-realisation, there is joy, freedom, clarity and grace.

To activate the soul blueprint for yourself and others, you can facilitate the healing process below.

ACTIVATION

Take a moment to consciously connect to your breath. Allow the breath to flow in and out and let yourself relax as you bring your awareness completely into this moment.

Ground yourself. Feel and intend that you are fully aware of your feet, and every way that your feet make contact with the earth. If you cannot sense that, then choose any part of your body to focus upon, feeling the earth energies of flesh and bone, muscle, blood and sensation, that help you connect with your body. Let the contact between the earth and your body feel palpable for you.

Stretch and move your jaw. Gently stretch your neck and throat by moving your head in various directions. Then relax.

Imagine, feel, visualise or intend that there are strings within your heart, as though your heart was a sacred instrument of the luminous realms of Spirit. See, sense, hear, imagine, feel or pretend that your heartstrings are being played by the gentle hand of Spirit, helping you remember and embody your true nature. Allow this to be a gentle experience, a soft remembering of the real you. Rest in this process for some moments.

If you wish to empower the process further, make spontaneous sounds, as though the vibration of your heartstrings is sending sound out through your throat. If you can feel those vibrations, you may like to dance, move, make shapes or even take yoga postures that feel authentic and resonant in the moment.

If you wish to work with a mantra, you can do so. I suggest the Tibetan Buddhist mantra for cleansing, protection and empowerment. Say, whisper or sing this mantra with a sense of peace, love and sacred offering for all beings in your heart. You can repeat it once, or any number of times that feels good for you. As you repeat the mantra, have a sense of all beings aligning in joyful harmony with their unique divine destiny—including you!

OM AH HUNG

(sounds like OHM - AH - HOONG)

When you are ready, say this prayer aloud:

For the spiritual benefit of all beings, I AM. I allow the spiritual intervention of divine grace to recalibrate, realign, heal and renew me. I am empowered as I surrender to my authentic soul path. Beloved and enlightened beings of compassion, please support me in awakening completely, with mercy and grace, for the spiritual benefit of all beings. OM AH HUNG.

If you wish to pray, write, sing, dance, facilitate an oracle card reading, or engage in another creative activity or movement at this time, you are encouraged to do so as a way of integrating the process further.

Rest, ground and hydrate yourself as you are ready.

You have completed your healing activation process.

You can trust your healing journey and the often hidden, yet always loving, higher purpose behind things happening as they do.

You are strong, and you shall flourish on all levels.

You shall heal. Do not give up. Proceed until you are exactly
where you most want to be.

You have the inner spiritual strength to ensure even a negative experience will only cause positive growth in you and your life.

The light can and will help me transform even the most difficult struggles into sacred paths of grace. Healing shall manifest completely, generously and lovingly, according to divine timing, for the spiritual benefit of all beings.

I AM grateful, strong and blessed.

It's time to be kind. Question and heal any guilt or shame that may
have prevented you from enjoying the natural pleasures of your body.
You are encouraged to enjoy the gift of your life.

Your delight can be a source of positive energy for yourself and others.

Reflect on what brings you joy and pleasure in such a way that it slows you down and helps you be present.

May I know the delight, pleasure, sensuality and sacred beauty which
will bring peace to my heart and set my soul free.

Changes in your life, including closing doors or missed opportunities, are not going to derail your fulfilment. Realignments are happening based on divine wisdom and timing. Trust in how your life path is unfolding.

When we are more open to life, the path to fruition becomes more accessible and direct. When we connect with our authentic path, we can access the abundant spiritual support available to us.

*True guidance may arise as a no, or a not right now, or as a yes
and go for it. When we are in the heart, we will clearly sense such
guidance and take comfort in it, rather than fight against it.*

You have what it takes. You are a light bearer.

*Tap the healing power and spiritual wisdom within you, to find
your way through any confusion or doubt. Have confidence in
yourself and know you are enough.*

My voice knows how to heal and release itself from judgement and fear. As I drop into my heart and trust my voice, I naturally evolve into a joyful and free expression of my divine potential, for the highest good of all.

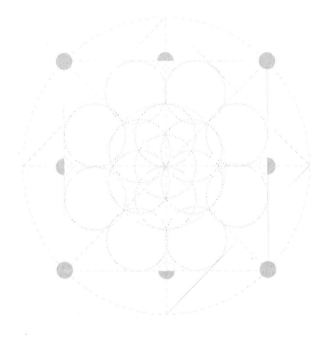

Expect an affirming YES from the Universe.

Your inner light shall continue to shine bright, no matter what is happening around you.

Trust in the goodness of the inevitable blessing of your destiny falling into place.

A heartfelt wish is going to manifest.

Love is the most powerful consciousness on the planet. It is also highly intelligent and attracts positive solutions and inspired pathways. Connect with the love of your beautiful heart and know that resolution will manifest.

We may feel we are bumbling along, yet we are blessed. An invisible and powerful field of grace moves with us, ensuring that our actions yield the best outcomes and that we attract what we truly want and need.

The heart has access to wisdom more powerful than logic and which can overcome any obstacle. To enter into that wisdom, we have to trust in something greater than our opinions and our allegiance to our history.

*To believe that history must repeat itself, or that what we
imagine is the limit of what can happen, is to deny the power of
the heart and the generosity of divine grace.*

Your radical and inspired heart dares to invite the most outlandishly blessed interventions of the light to benefit all beings. You have it within your heart to be a prayer alchemist for humanity.

YOUR BODY IS YOUR SACRED INSTRUMENT

Beneath the forms that captivate our minds, our great Universe is singing a cosmic love song. That sacred song of life is imbued with every nuance of feeling, encapsulating every experience with compassion. Every cell in existence is singing its particular note in this tremendous song. Aligning with the Universe, with our true nature and purpose, could be considered a tuning of ourselves to our true soul note, so that we can faithfully sing our part in the celestial choir.

Some see the body and soul as separate, but that is not my experience. I feel that the soul is born of the integration of spirit and body and that it emerges as a unique field, growing through lifetimes. The body is part of the soul, as is the spirit. Yet whilst the body eventually disintegrates, and the spirit is eternal, the soul is the divine feminine part of us that lives, evolves and expresses its divine potential through courageous and unique life journeys, lifetime after lifetime.

We are blessed with bodies as sacred instruments capable of experiencing so much. A beautiful teaching in the Buddhist tradition, refers to 'precious human existence'. It acknowledges each human lifetime as a miraculous happening and a profound and unmatched opportunity for spiritual awakening. The body is the vessel—the boat that carries us across the waters of samsara (suffering) and toward freedom. The body is a sacred instrument for spiritual enlightenment and the soul healing that so often forms part of that process.

In this exercise, we work with the body as our instrument. If you can play other musical instruments (or pots and pans with a certain creative flair!) then feel free to do so. But, remember what you use to play any instrument—your body!

The following exercise can be adapted to suit your circumstances and situation. From the previous exercises, we learned that holding joy and generosity as an intention in the heart can create healing through sound. We aim not to disturb but even boisterous, joyful abandon can become liberating when love is at its core.

YOUR SACRED INSTRUMENT

AUTHENTIC NATURAL TONING

Toning, or sounding, utilises voice as natural expression. It arises from within, as an exploration that is not cultivated but simply allowed to surface. I use the term 'authentic natural toning' to differentiate it from the skill of taught toning practices. This exercise is about dropping from the head into the heart and listening to the body, allowing it to speak to you without words through sounds.

If you wish to add or substitute body percussion—using hands, legs, feet or so on—to make sounds, please do so. Be kind to your body. Work with what feels authentic rather than what you think will look, or even sound, best. Let it be playful and exploratory. You can introduce other instruments if you wish.

Remember to keep your intention aligned with your heart and to share the sounds as an offering. To facilitate this, you can say:

May this work generate blessings, healing and liberation for the spiritual benefit of all beings. I ask for the Enlightened Ones of Love and Wisdom to protect and direct the energies for the greater good.

Is there a feeling you need to express? You may have the courage to allow your body to speak and be surprised by what arises. You could use toning to mourn a loss, to express delight and beauty and sensuality, or to experience the freedom of not having to voice anything other than the spontaneity of the moment. If this is new or uncomfortable for you, be kind, be gentle and go slow. Do not attempt to force a performance. Be with the process as your body learns to trust your mind and that you are capable of receiving without judgement or fear. At the same time, your mind comes to trust the wisdom of your body, and that it knows how to process experience and heal when given the chance to do so.

When you feel that you have expressed your soul through the instrument of your body, you can finish the process with this prayer:

May the energy created through this sacred play generate healing and spiritual benefit for all beings. So be it.

EMPOWERING MANTRA WITH BHAKTI (DEVOTION OF THE HEART)

Mantra is a powerful practice of sacred sound. Sourced from the wisdom of great sages, mantras have been passed down faithfully over thousands of years, providing acoustic medicine to heal mind body and soul. The intention and effects of mantras vary greatly. They can be used for gaining prosperity, finding true love, protection from negativities and awakening spiritual enlightenment. They are also a source of healing and blessing for oneself and all beings.

The Indian mystic Ramakrishna taught that the best path for securing spiritual progress is bhakti—the path of divine love and devotion. There are many ways that complex teachings can be misunderstood and distorted, but love is love and cuts through all confusion.

To chant specific mantras from the heart, with a sense of love and devotion, not only purifies the soul, it strengthens the heart and attracts all manner of positivity, blessings, protection. It advances the soul toward spiritual enlightenment and feels wonderful. It can be far easier to drop into a beautiful sound, chanted or sung with joy, than to master the meditative arts from more technical approaches. When devotion is strong enough, the courage that arises within the heart can allow us to conquer any obstacle and grow in confidence and competence.

I have chosen a simple mantra, based on a beautiful story about a wise old sage who was revered across many lands for his spiritual wisdom, power and kindness. He left his journal, the prayers he said faithfully every day, to his most advanced student. He told his student that he could only read and share the teachings in his journal when he left his body in a state of enlightenment, as they would then be proven to be effective. The student faithfully adhered to the master's wishes, and upon his enlightened passing, he opened the master's journal. Across every page was emblazoned one word, repeated as if for eternity—Rama.

Rama, or Lord Ram, is a Lord of Divine Love in the Hindu tradition. If, for a moment, we were to use a Christian lens, Ram could be said to be the Universal Christ Consciousness as it manifested in a divine being in India. Rama is an avatar of the God Vishnu, the aspect of the Hindu trinity connected to love, abundance, preservation and spiritual enlightenment through the heart.

This beautiful mantra invokes divine love, bliss, wisdom, enlightenment, love and the courage to discover and embrace the adventure of our spiritual path. It brings out the best in ourselves and helps us heal and attain our divine destiny. Say this simple mantra to balance your masculine and feminine sides and attract pure love into your life. It goes like this:

OM RAM RAMAYA NAMAHA
(sounds like OHM RAHM RAHM-AHH-YAH NAHM-AH-HAH)

If you are under twenty-nine years of age, you can substitute Namaha with Swaha (SWAH-HAH) instead.

You can play with singing this mantra or chanting it until it becomes so familiar that you begin to play with opening your heart and chanting it with love and devotion. To facilitate this process, you may want to imagine the most divinely loving being you can fathom gazing at you with unconditional divine love and adoration as you sing the name of that divine being, receiving and sharing that love.

You can do this as often as you wish. When you have chanted to your heart's content, you can complete your process with this simple prayer:

May these sounds of divine love reach through all dimensions and bring spiritual benefit to all beings, through divine grace, compassion and wisdom, so be it.

You do not need to force anything. Love holds space for all experiences.
You can rest in that sacred holding of the heart.

You do not have to contrive your happiness, but you can dip into the bliss
within your body to lighten your mental state and remind yourself that
everything is working out beautifully, according to a higher plan.

Be persistent on your path, but be gentle with yourself.

If you cannot proceed along a certain course, find another way.
Do not abandon your dreams. Things may not go to plan,
but they are still going to work out.

Take time to clean your heart and mind of negativity by focusing on the divine beings that bring joy to your heart.

*It is appropriate for you to desire personal and sacred space and
to access it in ways that support you.*

When we are thirsty, we do not reach for an empty glass;
we reach for one that is full. Seek nourishment from the sacred source
that can truly provide what you need.

*Let your heart relax. Allow the spiritual grace that wishes to reorder your
life to manifest its miraculous magic.*

You will experience peace, love and deep connection with your true self and the Universe. Good things are on their way to you.

As we choose to align our actions with our heart's truth,
we become the spiritual birth mothers and founding fathers of a
more spiritually advanced humanity.

If you attempt to fit into social constructs or cliques that don't reflect your essence, you will weaken yourself and become more susceptible to negativity. You are encouraged to consider what is natural and best for you and to be honest and authentic.

You have wisdom in your divinely alchemical heart.
You shall arise with dignity.

I assume full responsibility for myself and my life path. I call upon the enlightened heart of the Universe to assist me in manifesting my divine potential through grace, mercy and love, for the greatest spiritual benefit of all beings.

No matter how large a challenge may loom, you can continue to grow your spiritual connection, so it is always more potent than anything else.

Steady your heart and mind by placing your awareness and trust in the light,
and you shall attract protection, blessing and healing in abundance.